BL: 1. 2
AR PTS: 0.5

SUPER CUTE!

Baby Deer

by Bethany Olson

BLASTOFF! READERS

BELLWETHER MEDIA • MINNEAPOLIS, MN

Note to Librarians, Teachers, and Parents:

Blastoff! Readers are carefully developed by literacy experts and combine standards-based content with developmentally appropriate text.

Level 1 provides the most support through repetition of high-frequency words, light text, predictable sentence patterns, and strong visual support.

Level 2 offers early readers a bit more challenge through varied simple sentences, increased text load, and less repetition of high-frequency words.

Level 3 advances early-fluent readers toward fluency through increased text and concept load, less reliance on visuals, longer sentences, and more literary language.

Level 4 builds reading stamina by providing more text per page, increased use of punctuation, greater variation in sentence patterns, and increasingly challenging vocabulary.

Level 5 encourages children to move from "learning to read" to "reading to learn" by providing even more text, varied writing styles, and less familiar topics.

Whichever book is right for your reader, Blastoff! Readers are the perfect books to build confidence and encourage a love of reading that will last a lifetime!

This edition first published in 2014 by Bellwether Media, Inc.

No part of this publication may be reproduced in whole or in part without written permission of the publisher. For information regarding permission, write to Bellwether Media, Inc., Attention: Permissions Department, 5357 Penn Avenue South, Minneapolis, MN 55419.

Library of Congress Cataloging-in-Publication Data

Olson, Bethany.
 Baby deer / by Bethany Olson.
    p. cm. – (Blastoff! readers. Super cute!)
 Audience: K to grade 3.
 Summary: "Developed by literacy experts for students in kindergarten through grade three, this book introduces baby deer to young readers through leveled text and related photos"– Provided by publisher.
 Includes bibliographical references and index.
 ISBN 978-1-60014-925-2 (hardcover : alk. paper)
 1. Fawns–Juvenile literature. 2. Deer–Juvenile literature. 3. Animals–Infancy–Juvenile literature. I. Title.
 QL737.U55O398 2014
 599.65'139–dc23

                                                            2013007815

Printed in the United States of America, North Mankato, MN.

Table of Contents

Fawn!

A baby deer
is called a fawn.
It lives in the forest.

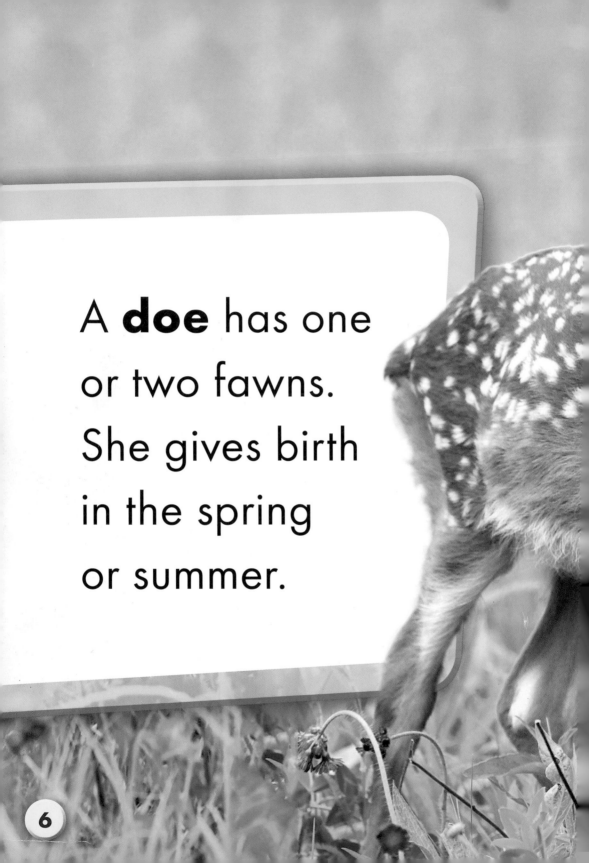

A **doe** has one or two fawns. She gives birth in the spring or summer.

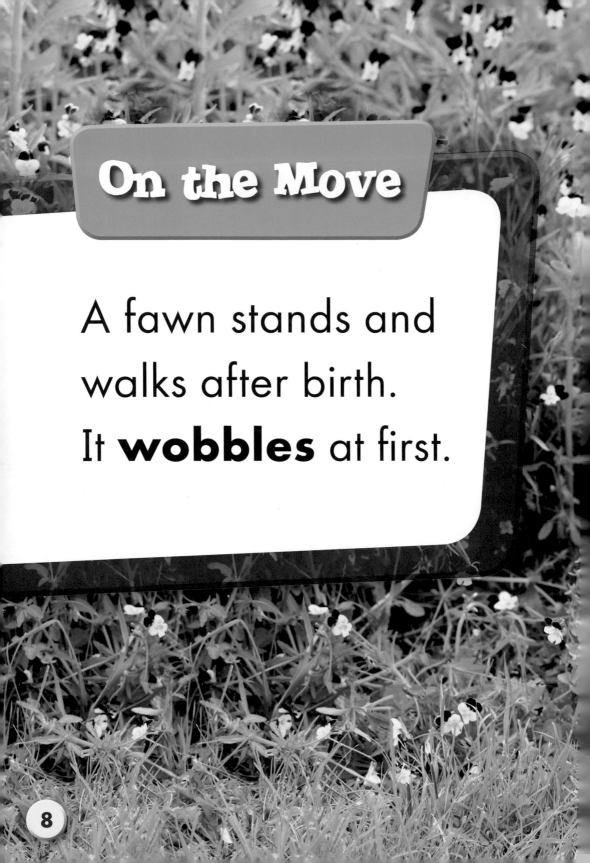

On the Move

A fawn stands and walks after birth. It **wobbles** at first.

The fawn follows mom. It is thirsty for her milk.

Mom **grooms** her fawn. She licks its fur clean.

Time to Hide

Mom leaves to **forage** for food. Now the fawn is alone.

The fawn stays
in tall grasses.
Its spots help
it hide.

It drops to the ground when a **predator** is near.

Sometimes the fawn **bleats** when it is scared. Come back, mom!

Glossary

bleats—makes a noise that sounds like a shaky cry

doe—a female deer

forage—to search for grasses and other plants to eat

grooms—cleans

predator—an animal that hunts other animals for food

wobbles—moves in a shaky way

To Learn More

AT THE LIBRARY

Doudna, Kelly. *It's a Baby White-Tailed Deer!* Edina, Minn.: ABDO, 2008.

Kawa, Katie. *Fawns.* New York, N.Y.: Gareth Stevens Pub., 2012.

Springett, Martin. *Kate & Pippin: An Unlikely Love Story.* New York, N.Y.: Henry Holt, 2012.

ON THE WEB

Learning more about deer is as easy as 1, 2, 3.

1. Go to www.factsurfer.com

2. Enter "deer" into the search box.

3. Click the "Surf" button and you will see a list of related Web sites.

With factsurfer.com, finding more information is just a click away.

Index

The images in this book are reproduced through the courtesy of: Alaska Stock Images R. Collection: Alaskan Express/ Age Fotostock, front cover; Betty Shelton, pp. 4-5; ARCO/ Wittek, R. / Glow Images, pp. 6-7, 14-15; J & C Sohns/ Glow Images, pp. 8-9; Klein-Hubert/ Kimball Stock, pp. 10-11; Mike Criss/ Glow Images, pp. 12-13; Aflo Animal/ Glow Images, pp. 16-17; Arco Images/ Glow Images, pp. 18-19; Andrew Williams, pp. 20-21.